WEAPONS AND MACHINES IN WARFARE

WEAPONS AND MACHINES OF WORLD WAR II

Craig Boutland

Cavendish Square

Published in 2024 by Cavendish Square Publishing, LLC
2544 Clinton Street, Buffalo, NY 14224

Portions of this work were originally authored by Charlie Samuels and published as *Machines and Weaponry of World War II*. All new material this edition authored by Craig Boutland.

Design Manager: Keith Davis
Picture Manager: Sophie Mortimer

Picture Credits
Front Cover: Shutterstock: Stephen Meese
All photographs Robert Hunt Library Except: Mike Hoffman: 26; Shutterstock: Paul Drabot 19t, 41, Sergey Kamshylin 44, Maxim Lysenko 36, Stephen Meese 1, 7, Phantom 20, Trinacria Photo 30l, Rob Wilson 16; Thinkstock: Photos.com 14br; U.S. National Archives: 27tr, 35cr; John Woolford: 38, 44.
Key: t = top, c = center, b = bottom, l = left, r = right.

Cataloging-in-Publication Data

Names: Boutland, Craig.
Title: Weapons and machines of World War II / Craig Boutland.
Description: Buffalo, New York : Cavendish Square Publishing, 2024. | Series: Weapons and machines in warfare | Includes glossary and index.
Identifiers: ISBN 9781502669261 (pbk.) | ISBN 9781502669278 (library bound) | ISBN 9781502669285(ebook)
Subjects: LCSH: World War, 1939-1945--Equipment and supplies--Juvenile literature. | Military weapons--History--20th century--Juvenile literature.
Classification: LCC D743.7 B66 2024 | DDC 940.54'83--dc23

CPSIA compliance information: Batch #CSCSQ24: For further information contact Cavendish Square Publishing LLC at 1-877-980-4450.

Printed in the United States of America

CONTENTS

Introduction

After its defeat in World War I (1914–1918), Germany was forced to reduce the size of its armed forces. Then, in 1933, Adolf Hitler came to power in Germany. Under his rule, Germany began to rearm. In particular, it built tanks, submarines, and **dive bombers**. In 1939 and 1940, Germany's tanks and Stuka dive bombers helped it conquer much of northern Europe. Then its submarines, called U-boats, threatened to starve Britain into defeat.

The USS *Angler* was one of the Gato class of submarines. More than 300 vessels were built to the same template. It was the largest building program ever undertaken by the U.S. Navy.

dive bomber: A small bomber that approaches its target in a vertical dive.

"Tika IV" was a P-41 Mustang. The U.S. fighter was useful for long-range missions. Tanks beneath the wings carried extra fuel.

THE ALLIED RESPONSE

The Allies—Britain, France, the United States, and the Soviet Union—developed their own weapons. Many were built in the United States by women who replaced male workers in factories. In the Soviet Union, whole factories were moved east, away from the fighting, so they could keep making tanks, airplanes, and guns.

The Allies built long-range bombers that could strike at targets in Europe and the Pacific. They built fighter planes to protect them. In the Pacific, they built submarines to sink Japanese **merchant ships**, and they built aircraft carriers. These "floating islands" were key to victory. They brought the aerial war to Japan's home islands.

merchant ship: An unarmed cargo vessel used for trade.

A member of a British gun crew prepares to load a shell into a 25-pounder. Used shell casings lie on the ground behind the gun.

25-pounder

Artillery support is key in modern warfare, and from 1940 the British Army had the benefit of one of the most reliable field guns ever made. The Ordnance QF (quick firing) 25-pounder got its name from the weight of its ammunition. The 25-pounder had a circular firing platform so the gun could turn in any direction. It could even be aimed into the air, so it could also be used as a **howitzer**. It was loved by its crews and feared by the enemy.

howitzer: An artillery gun that fires shells in a high arc to pass over enemy defenses.

A POPULAR GUN

The 25-pounder was popular with gunners because it was reliable and didn't break down easily. It was suitable for all types of environments, including the deserts of North Africa.

The 25-pounder was highly mobile. Early models were towed by trucks or tractors, but later models were **self-propelled**. The gun had a high rate of fire. When its six-person crew worked hard, it could fire six to eight rounds per minute. The gun's maximum range was 13,400 yards (12,253 m).

EYEWITNESS

"It has been said with some authority that the 25-pounder—the equipment which was to become the main weapon of Canadian field artillery. . . was the first piece of artillery to be developed logically from 'the target backwards.'"

Guy G. Simonds
Commander, Canadian Army, World War II

More than 12,000 25-pounders were produced during the war. The gun was used everywhere that British or Commonwealth forces fought.

self-propelled: For guns, able to move on their own through the use of an engine and wheels or tracks.

Aircraft Carrier

During World War II, the aircraft carrier became the key weapon in naval warfare. The so-called "flat tops" formed floating airfields. They carried dive bombers and torpedo bombers to sink enemy vessels and fighters to defend themselves. The sea war in the Pacific was won by the U.S. carrier fleets.

The USS *Enterprise* carried 90 aircraft. It had two **hydraulic** catapults to shoot the planes off the deck at a high enough speed for takeoff.

hydraulic: Powered by energy created by putting liquids under pressure.

A fighter plane flies above the USS *Enterprise*. Ropes across the deck caught hooks beneath the aircraft to stop the planes as they landed.

TURNING POINT

When the Japanese attacked **Pearl Harbor** in Hawai'i in December 1941, none of the eight U.S. carriers were at the base. By the end of the war, more than 30 carriers led the U.S. challenge to Japanese control of the Pacific.

EYEWITNESS

"Through the skill and devotion to duty of their armed forces of all branches in the Midway area our citizens can now rejoice that a momentous victory is in the making."

Chester W. Nimitz
Admiral of the U.S. Fleet

The turning point of the Pacific War came at the Battle of Midway in June 1942. The Japanese wrongly thought the U.S. carriers had been sunk a month earlier. At Midway, 37 U.S. carrier bombers destroyed two Japanese carriers. Soon after, two more Japanese carriers were destroyed. The carriers had brought U.S. domination in the Pacific.

Pearl Harbor: The base of the US Pacific Fleet in Hawaii, attacked by Japan on December 7, 1941.

The Flying Fortress had a crew of 10. The pilot and copilot were joined by an engineer, a navigator, a **bombardier**, a radio operator, and four gunners.

B-17 Flying Fortress

The B-17 not only carried a lethal payload of bombs to drop on the enemy; it also bristled with 13 Browning machine guns to defend itself against enemy fighters. This heavy defensive armament led to the nickname "Flying Fortress." B-17s began their raids on Germany in August 1942, and 8,680 machines of the most successful variant, the B-17G, were built. These machines pounded enemy positions until the end of the war.

bombardier: The member of a bomber crew whose job is to aim and drop the aircraft's bombs.

FIGHTER PROTECTION

The Flying Fortress was extremely popular with pilots. It was reliable and easy to maneuver, and it could survive heavy fire. Its range varied from 3,770 miles (6,034 km) unloaded to 1,110 miles (1,760 km) fully loaded with bombs.

EYEWITNESS

“In my opinion the B-17 was the finest combat airplane the Air Force has ever had. It was capable of carrying much more weight than we ever put into it: the problem was the configuration of the bomb bay.”

Lt. John Minahan
U.S. 19th Bomb Group, Mareeba, Australia, 1942

Even with their strong armor and heavy firepower, the slow bombers risked being shot down. After 60 out of 291 planes were shot down during raids over southern Germany on October 14, 1943, unaccompanied bombing missions were halted. For protection, the bombers flew in tight formation with a fighter escort.

Ground crew prepare to start the propellors of a B-17 before it takes off from an airfield in Great Britain.

B-17s fly in formation toward Germany on one of the “1,000-bomber” raids on German cities.

ground crew: The mechanics who maintain an airplane and prepare it for flights.

B-29 Superfortress

Development of the B-29 began in 1940. At that time, World War II was raging in Europe, but the U.S. had not yet entered the war. The U.S. Air Force decided it needed a long-range bomber that could reach Europe if necessary. The new bomber deserved its "super" nickname. The huge machine was twice the weight of a B-17 and had a range of 3,250 miles (5,200 km). Engineers had to develop a **pressurized** cabin as standard so the crew could operate at the high altitudes it flew.

Ground crew in the Marianas Islands prepare a Superfortress for a mission over Japan. The Superfortress could carry 20,000 pounds (9,075 kg) of bombs.

pressurized: Made safe and comfortable by pumping air in.

A formation of Superfortresses flies past Mount Fuji, a volcano in the middle of Japan that is an important symbol of the Japanese homeland.

BOMBING JAPAN

The B-29's long range made it vital in the Pacific. In the summer of 1944, the capture of Saipan in the Marianas brought the Japanese home islands within range. B-29s flew nighttime raids to bomb Japan. Wooden cities such as Tokyo burned in huge firestorms. Many thousands of people were killed.

The most famous B-29 was called *Enola Gay*. On August 6, 1945, it dropped the first atomic bomb, "Little Boy," on the city of Hiroshima. Three days later, another B-29 called *Bockscar* dropped a second bomb called "Fat Man" on Nagasaki. The Japanese surrendered a few weeks later.

EYEWITNESS

"If **Dante** had been with us on the plane, he would have been terrified."

Paul Tibbets
Commander, Enola Gay, on bombing of Hiroshima

Dante: Italian writer who wrote a poem about Hell.

Bren Gun

The Bren gun was usually supported by a bipod or tripod. Its curved **magazine** held 30 rounds.

The Bren was designed to give support to an infantry section. It was named after the Czech armaments factory at Brno—where much of the development took place—and the British ordnance center at Enfield. Infantrymen liked the Bren because it was light and very accurate. It used the same .303 ammunition as the standard British rifle, the Lee-Enfield. The Bren gun was fitted with a magazine that only took 30 rounds. This meant the gun had to be reloaded frequently.

British gunners in Tobruk, Libya, use a Bren gun to fire at Axis aircraft. British and Commonwealth troops were besieged in the North African port for 240 days in 1941.

magazine: A metal case loaded with a number of cartridges ready to be clipped into a machine gun.

ACCURATE AT RANGE

The Bren gun had a two-man team; one man fired and the other reloaded. All infantry units were equipped with a Bren gun, and all of the men in the unit shared the task of carrying the ammunition. The gun was useful because of its long range. It was accurate up to 600 yards (550 m), with a maximum range of 1,850 yards (1,700 m). Later models were supported on a bipod or a tripod. This helped them become even more accurate, as they were more stable.

GUN CARRIER

The Bren gun carrier was a lightly armored tracked vehicle used to carry infantry into battle even under enemy fire. It was the most widely used **armored fighting vehicle** (AFV) among the Allied Forces.
The three-man crew fired a Bren gun mounted in front of the vehicle.

A British infantryman fires a Bren gun in northern France in 1944. Canada, Australia, and India also produced Bren guns for their forces.

armored fighting vehicle: A military vehicle protected by armor and equipped with weapons.

C-47 Skytrain

Allied senior officers all agreed that the C-47 Skytrain, or Dakota, was vital in winning the war. However, it did not carry bombs or try to engage enemy positions. Adapted from a passenger jet, the Douglas DC-3, this transport plane allowed the U.S. military to move men and supplies quickly to where they were needed. It saw service worldwide.

A key role of the Skytrain was to fly over the Himalayas from India to China. The planes took supplies to Chinese nationalists and U.S. Air Force bases. Pilots called the mountain range "the Hump."

transport plane: An aircraft that is adapted to carry large amounts of cargo or soldiers.

Soldiers climb into a C-47 Dakota for a practice jump. The Dakota nickname came from Douglas Aircraft Company Transport Aircraft: DACoTA.

FLEXIBLE WORKHORSE

The Skytrain could carry 6,000 pounds (13,200 kg) of cargo, including a jeep or a 37mm cannon, or 28 men in combat gear. It was used to drop paratroopers and for **reconnaissance**. For medical airlift, it had room for 14 stretcher patients and three nurses. With its reinforced floor, larger freight doors, and a more powerful engine than the civilian plane, the C-47 was a workhorse. It had a range of 3,800 miles (6,080 km).

EYEWITNESS

"Probably the most memorable thing about the [Dakota] was the smell. The odor of the leather mixed with hydraulic fluid made a perfume second to none. [The plane] always treated me well...and my memories of it are all good."

Tex Gehman
Canadian C-47 pilot, World War II

A mechanic services a C-47 engine. The two engines were more powerful than those fitted to the civilian model of the airplane.

reconnaissance: Gathering information by surveying enemy positions and strength.

Two Hurricanes fly in formation. When it entered service in 1937, the Hurricane became the RAF's first **monoplane** fighter.

Hurricane

The Hawker Hurricane changed the future of fighter planes. It was the workhorse of British airpower in the aerial battles of 1940. In the **Battle of Britain**, the RAF had 32 squadrons of Hurricanes and only 19 of the more famous Spitfires. During the battle, Hurricanes shot down more than 80 percent of the planes lost by the Germans.

 monoplane: An aircraft with one wing on either side.

CANVAS BODY

The Hurricane was super strong. The framework of its body was made from steel tubing. This was covered in canvas. That meant that it could withstand damage that would destroy most fighters. With eight machine guns on its wings, Hurricane could fire 150 bullets per second.

As the war went on, the Hurricane was used less as a fighter and more as a bomber. The Mark II was an improved fighter–bomber. In the Mediterranean and North Africa, it was used to attack vehicles on the ground with rockets, bombs, and added guns.

EYEWITNESS

"It was a delightful aeroplane—not as agile as a Spitfire, but it had a very good gun platform. It was very steady and took a tremendous amount of battle damage without appearing to worry too much."

RGA Barclay
Pilot officer, RAF

Pilots run to get their Hurricanes airborne during the Battle of Britain in 1940.

There were special versions of the Hurricane developed for use in the desert, in tropical conditions, or at sea.

Battle of Britain: The air battle between the RAF and the Luftwaffe over England in 1940.

Katyusha

One of the most feared Soviet weapons of World War II was a mobile rocket launcher. The weapon was named for a popular song, Katyusha, or "little Katy." It could fire multiple rockets at the same time. Although not very accurate, it unleashed awesome firepower from vehicles like tanks or trucks.

One advantage of the Katyusha was that it was light and easy to move. Trucks could be positioned to deliver a devastating **barrage** on a target.

barrage: A large amount of shells or bombs delivered on one place at the same time.

Rockets streak into the night sky toward German positions from a whole row of Katyushas mounted on top of tracked tractors.

MULTIPLE LAUNCHER

The Katyusha could carry up to 48 launching pipes. There were several versions. The most common was the BM-13. It had a range of 5.29 miles (8.47 km). Its rockets weighed 93 pounds (42 kg) and were nearly 6 feet (180 cm) long.

A distinguishing feature of the Katyusha was a distinctive whine it made when a rocket was launched. The sound demoralized the Germans. It sounded a little like a church organ, so the Germans nicknamed the weapon "Stalin's Organ."

NAMED FOR A GIRL

The Katyusha's unusual nickname came from a popular Soviet wartime song, "Katyusha." The song is about a girl who is missing her boyfriend while he is away fighting in the war. The association may have begun because the rockets were all stamped with the letter K for the factory where they were made.

rocket: A missile that is powered by its own fuel and propulsion unit.

Ten versions of the Lancaster were produced, but none of them was very different from the original 1942 model.

Lancaster Bomber

Early in World War II, British bombers were twin-engined machines, but it became clear that bigger aircraft were needed. In 1942, the four-engined Avro Lancaster entered service. It became the main aircraft used in the RAF's campaign of night raids on German cities. Its 33-foot (10 m) long bomb bay allowed it to carry huge bombs. Tallboys were 5-ton (5,445 kg) "earthquake bombs." Lancasters also sank the famous German **battleship**, *Tirpitz*, in November 1944.

battleship: The most heavily armed type of warship.

RAIDING THE DAMS

The most famous Lancaster mission was the Dambusters raid of 1943. The targets were dams in Germany's Ruhr Valley. The Lancasters of 617 Squadron carried special "bouncing bombs." The bombs skipped along the surface of the lakes behind the dams, then sank and blew up next to the dam wall. To get the bombs to bounce, the pilots had to fly just 60 feet (18 m) above the water at 240 miles per hour (390 km/h).

EYEWITNESS

"I felt a little remote and unreal sitting up there in the warm **cockpit** of my Lancaster, watching this mighty power which we had unleashed..."

Guy Gibson
Squadron commander, Dambusters raid

A Lancaster is fueled and loaded with bombs. The bomber had a crew of seven men, including pilots, bombardiers, and gunners.

cockpit: The part of an airplane where the pilot and copilot sit.

Landing Craft Assault

When the Western Allies began to take the offensive in World War II in 1942, they needed to land troops quickly on hostile shores. The answer lay in special landing craft. These flat-bottomed boats had **ramps** that opened to allow troops on and off. Each landing craft had a crew of four and could carry up to 36 men.

U.S. soldiers and a Landing Craft Assault crew face a photographer as their craft nears the coast of Normandy, in the aftermath of D-Day.

ramp: A surface that can be raised or lowered to allow people to enter or leave.

British troops rush ashore from an LCA during a landing on a beach in North Africa during Operation Torch in November 1942.

D-DAY LANDINGS

In Europe, Landing Craft Assault (LCAs) were vital to the D-Day landings. They helped land 170,000 men on five beaches in Normandy in northern France on June 6, 1944.

A total of 4,000 landing craft were used to ferry men from warships off the French coast to the beaches. The crews faced heavy fire. Some found it difficult to land in the right place. Some soldiers had to wade ashore through deep water when their landing craft could not reach the beaches. Still, in the first 16 hours, 130,000 men managed to get ashore.

AMTRACKS

In the Pacific, the U.S. landing at Tawara in November 1943 went badly wrong. A very low tide meant that the LCAs got caught on reefs as they approached the shore. As a result, the U.S. Navy began using special "amtracks." These **amphibious** tractors had propellers to drive through water and caterpillar tracks to cross reefs.

amphibious: Something that can operate on land or in the water.

One of the few surviving Liberty ships is the *Jeremiah O'Brien*. All the ships were built to the same **template**, so they looked identical.

Liberty Ship

In 1941, the survival of Britain was in doubt because of German U-boat attacks on the shipping boats that carried supplies to the island nation. At this point, U.S. shipyards set about one of the biggest industrial programs ever. They aimed to replace and increase the number of cargo ships available to cross the Atlantic. The program was a huge success. Between 1941 and 1945, 18 U.S. shipyards built a remarkable 2,710 Liberty ships.

template: A plan that gives the shapes of pieces used in construction.

A female worker checks the welded seam between sections of a Liberty ship.

RECORDBREAKERS

In 1940, it took about 230 days to build a merchant ship. The Liberty ships could be built in just 42 days. One ship was built in just 4 days and 15.5 hours as a publicity stunt. Many of the workers were women who did the jobs formerly done by men. The ships were all built to the same plan. They were made of steel sections welded together. Welding was quicker than **riveting** the metal together.

FDR'S NAME

The Liberty ships got their name from U.S. president Franklin D. Roosevelt. He recalled a founder of the United States, Patrick Henry, who said, "Give me liberty or give me death!" Launching the ship-building program in September 1941, Roosevelt said "There must be liberty, worldwide and eternal." The ships were part of achieving that aim.

The USS *Robert E. Peary* was built as a publicity stunt in just 4.5 days. It was constructed in the yards of Henry Kaiser, who oversaw the Liberty ship program.

riveting: A method of joining pieces of metal together with flat-headed bolts.

M-2 Flamethrower

Flamethrowers were used to destroy infantry holed up in concrete bunkers or thick undergrowth. All the combatant nations used them during World War II. They were dangerous to use. The U.S. M-2 used a tank of **flammable** nitrogen that was strapped to the back of the flamethrower carrier. The U.S. Army Chemical Warfare Service developed flamethrowers between 1940 and 1941. The early M-1 was crude and unreliable. Finally, the M-2 was introduced in the summer of 1944 and first used on Guam.

This U.S. infantryman is carrying an M-2 flamethrower on a Pacific island. The weapon was useful against enemies who hid in thick vegetation.

flammable: Something that catches fire and burns easily.

FLAMETHROWER

Unlike the M-1, the M-2 did not rely on electrical **ignition**. Instead, it used special cartridges to light the gas. The cartridges were stored in a drum at the tip of the flame tube.

EYEWITNESS

"Womack then aimed the nozzle at the opening made by the 75mm gun. He pressed the trigger. With a whoooooosh the flame leaped at the opening. Some muffled screams, then all was quiet."

Corporal Eugene B Sledge
1st Marine Division

U.S. Marine units used a tactic called "corkscrew and blowtorch." They used heavy machine fire to allow flamethrowers to get close to their targets. The weapon could fire flames in bursts of about 7 seconds. At a range of 20 to 40 yards (18 to 36 m), the flames would destroy everything. Later, flamethrowers were increasingly replaced by flamethrowing tanks.

A U.S. soldier uses an M-2 to set fire to a building that might shelter Japanese troops during fighting for Namur, one of the Marshall Islands.

ignition: The act of starting a machine by setting light to its fuel.

A U.S. paratrooper carries his M1 as his patrol uses a churchyard wall for shelter while searching a French village in June 1944.

M1 Garand Rifle

This rifle, soon nicknamed the "GI's best friend," was the first semiautomatic rifle to become standard issue for the U.S. military. It came into use in 1936. Although it was quite heavy to carry, soldiers liked it because it was accurate at long range, fired rapidly, and had little **recoil**. It was also highly reliable and rarely jammed.

The M1 was a standard weapon. More than 5.5 million were produced.

recoil: The force that pushes a gun backward when it fires.

SEMIAUTOMATIC RIFLE

The M1 was a semiautomatic. That meant that the gas given off by firing a round pushed the next round into the chamber from a clip of eight or ten powerful .30 Springfield bullets. The gun fired a round every time the trigger was pulled, up to 30 rounds per minute. That gave U.S. soldiers a clear advantage over the bolt-action rifles with which their enemies were usually armed. The Garand had a range of about 440 yards (400 m). More than 6.25 million M1 rifles were manufactured before they were finally taken out of service in the early 1960s.

EYEWITNESS

"In my opinion, the M1 rifle is the greatest implement of battle ever devised."

George S. Patton
Commander, U.S. Third Army

U.S. soldiers load their M1s under cover during a **firefight** with Germans in northern France.

firefight: A close-range gunfight in which both sides fire at the other.

P-47 Thunderbolt

The P-47 was the heaviest single-engine fighter of World War II. It weighed in at 8 tons (7.9 tonnes) and was certainly not easy to fly. American pilots named this Republic Aviation Thunderbolt "the Jug," while the British said the nickname was short for "juggernaut." During the later campaigns of World War II, however, the Thunderbolt really came into its own by attacking ground targets.

A P-47 Thunderbolt (front) escorts a B-17 Flying Fortress. Escort duty was one of the main tasks for the P-47.

juggernaut: A name for a massive, slow-moving truck.

Ground crew prepare belts of shells to load into a Thunderbolt's eight machine guns.

The P-47's propeller was a giant 12 feet (3.65 m) across.

TWO ROLES

The Thunderbolt had two main roles. It was an effective escort plane that could take on enemy fighters in high-altitude dogfights. It was also an outstanding ground-attack aircraft. As a fighter-bomber, it could carry up to 2,500 pounds (1,135 kg) of bombs or rockets. Its eight 0.5-caliber machine guns could **strafe** targets on the ground. The whole aircraft was solid enough to withstand damage. The cockpit was armored so that the pilot had additional protection.

DIVE BOMBER

The Germans' most effective ground-attack aircraft was the JU-87 Stuka. In the lightning attacks of the Blitzkrieg at the start of the war, the plane would dive almost vertically to release its bombs. A siren on its leg gave out a wail that terrified people on the ground. A bent "gull wing" made the airplane better at diving and easier to maneuver. The acceleration of diving could make the pilot black out. The airplane had special air brakes that would bring it out of its dive if that happened.

strafe: To fire from the air at targets on the ground.

Underwing fuel tanks meant that Mustangs based in Britain could escort bombers all the way to the German capital, Berlin, and back.

Mustang

American P-51 Mustangs destroyed 4,950 enemy aircraft in the European theater. This was the highest **strike rate** of any U.S. fighter. The original Mustang design was supplemented by two successful additions: the Rolls Royce Merlin engine and the drop tanks that vastly extended its range. Nearly 15,000 Mustangs were built.

EYEWITNESS

"The thing that really set the Mustang apart from any other fighter, friend or foe, was its range. With a 75-gallon tank slung under each wing, it could perform the unheard-of: It could fly six-hour missions."

Capt. Robert Goebel
31st Fighter group, Twelfth Airforce

strike rate: The average number of enemy aircraft shot down per fighter.

Andrew D. Turner was one of the Tuskegee Airmen—the only Black pilots who flew in the U.S. Army Corps while the military services were still segregated.

LONGER RANGE

The Mustang's great advantage over other fighters was its range. It could fly 908 miles (1,500 km), which took it deep into enemy territory. The Mustang escorted U.S. bombers on raids on Germany's industrial heartland. The fighter was armed with six 12.7mm Browning machine guns fixed in its wings. It could be used as a dive bomber, bomber escort, ground-attacker, or interceptor. It was far superior to anything the Germans possessed. Hermann Goering was the head of the **Luftwaffe**. He said that when he saw Mustangs over Berlin, he knew Germany had lost the war.

The first Mustang was an average machine. The addition of a Rolls Royce engine turned it into what many say was the best fighter of the war.

Luftwaffe: The official name of Germany's air force.

The round drum magazine of the PPSh-41 could hold 35 rounds of ammunition. Holes in the sides of the barrel helped keep the gun cool.

PPSh-41 Submachine Gun

Submachine guns had first been used late in World War I. They were inaccurate over long ranges, but gave great firepower close up. The PPSh-41 was a Soviet submachine gun produced in huge numbers for the Red Army from 1941. It was reliable and needed little cleaning. It was ideal for **conscripts** to use and for fighting in urban areas or at close quarters.

ENEMY WEAPONS

The German Army recognized the great qualities of the PPSh. They captured so many during their invasion of the Soviet Union that they were able to use them against their enemies, including Soviet forces. The Germans began a program to convert the captured guns to use the standard German submachine gun round, the 9mm Parabellum.

conscripts: Untrained civilians who are forced to serve in the army.

Soviet infantry at a victory parade are seen carrying the PPSh-41 submachine guns that gave them awesome firepower.

This Russian **partisan** carries a PPSh-41. The weapon was ideal for partisans because it was easy to maintain.

MASS PRODUCTION

The gun had to be cheap and quick to produce. It used a new technology called metal pressing, so only the barrel and the drum magazine were expensive. Between 1941 and 1945, 5 million of the weapons were produced.

Like other Soviet weapons, the PPSh had to withstand freezing temperatures. It could fire at a rate of 900 rounds per minute. Although it was heavy to carry, it could fire 5,000 rounds before it needed to be cleaned.

partisan: Someone who fights in an armed resistance group in occupied territory.

The Sherman M4 was the most widely produced of all Allied tanks. More than 40,000 were built after it first appeared at El Alamein in October 1942.

Sherman Tank

When it first came into action in 1942, the U.S. M4 Sherman was a big improvement on all previous Allied **medium tanks**. After its baptism of fire in North Africa, the Sherman appeared wherever the Allies fought. It was produced in huge numbers. Some 30,000 Shermans saw action in Italy and western Europe as the standard Allied tank.

medium tank: A tank that is heavily armored but still light enough to move quickly.

FAST AND VERSATILE

Later versions of the tank were well armed with a 17-pounder (7.62 kg) gun that could take on Germany's heavy tanks at long range. Its powered **turret** allowed the crew to turn the gun and fire more quickly than the enemy.

EYEWITNESS

"[The Sherman] was fast and versatile, but poorly armoured, so we learnt to get our shots in first. Later, in France, I lost good friends who were unable to get out of blazing Shermans."

James Douglas Scott
Trooper, British Army

The Sherman had three advantages over German tanks: It was reliable and easy to fix; it was very strong; and it could be mass-produced quickly and cheaply. However, it had a weaker engine and gun, although the gun was later improved. Its narrow tracks meant that it could sink in soft ground. The Sherman also had a reputation for catching fire easily.

A Sherman rumbles ashore from a Landing Ship Tank (LST) in Normandy in the aftermath of D-Day, June 1944.

In Italy, a Sherman commander looks out over a valley as the Allies advance in 1943.

turret: The top part of a tank, which carries the main gun and can revolve.

Spitfire

Loved by its pilots and remembered as a key weapon during the Battle of Britain, the Supermarine Spitfire is the most famous of all British fighter planes. It was quicker than most other fighters and was easy to maneuver. That meant it could dodge gunfire in "dogfights" with enemy fighters. Cannon and Browning machine guns gave it serious firepower. The airplane was a major fighter in the Royal Air Force in World War II.

Spitfires fly above southern England in the summer of 1940. The Spitfire was a match for German fighters because of its great maneuverability.

dogfight: A one-on-one battle in which two fighter planes try to shoot each other down.

A surviving Spitfire takes to the air. There were various different models of the plane, which was originally designed by R. J. Mitchell.

INTO ACTION

The Spitfire made its **maiden flight** on March 5, 1940. It was the latest in aircraft technology. British air chiefs were so impressed, they ordered 370 to be built. Supermarine got them all ready in time to fight in the Battle of Britain later in the year.

EYEWITNESS

"When I was first given one to fly, my first emotion was almost intimidation. [The fighter] felt like a thoroughbred horse watching a new rider coming up. . . But once I was inside, the Spitfire, quite frankly, flew me."

Geoffrey Wellum
Squadron leader, RAF

The Spitfire was designed as a short-range fighter plane. It could carry two 250-pound (113 kg) bombs. It was also useful for photo reconnaissance, which was used extensively to locate enemy positions and to survey damage caused by bombing raids.

maiden flight: A term for a debut, or first, flight.

Submarine

During World War II, German *Unterseeboots*—U-boats—sought to sink Allied ships. The submarines would organize in "wolf packs" to hunt merchant convoys in the Atlantic. The most successful submarine campaign of the war, however, was in the Pacific. U.S. submarines made up less than 2 percent of the vessels of the U.S. Navy, but they sank more than 30 percent of Japan's surface fleet and strangled the Japanese war effort.

The USS *Nautilus* had a long range, so it was used as a tanker to take air fuel to island airbases. It was also used to get raiding forces ashore on **occupied** islands.

occupied: Controlled by the enemy.

A U.S. submarine captain uses a **periscope** to study the movement of ships on the surface of the ocean above his submarine.

UNDERWATER

When the United States entered the war after the attack on Pearl Harbor on December 7, 1941, there were only 14 working U.S. subs in the Pacific. Another 130 were built during the war. The Japanese relied on imports of oil, food, and other supplies. The U.S. campaign strangled the economy by sinking over 5 million tons of merchant shipping. The largest single victim was the aircraft carrier *Shinano*.

U-BOATS

German U-boats were the Nazis' most effective weapon in the Battle of the Atlantic. Germany's submarine fleet sank almost 3,000 Allied merchant ships. Its aim was to starve Britain into submission. As the war went on, the Allies got better at defending convoys against sub attack.

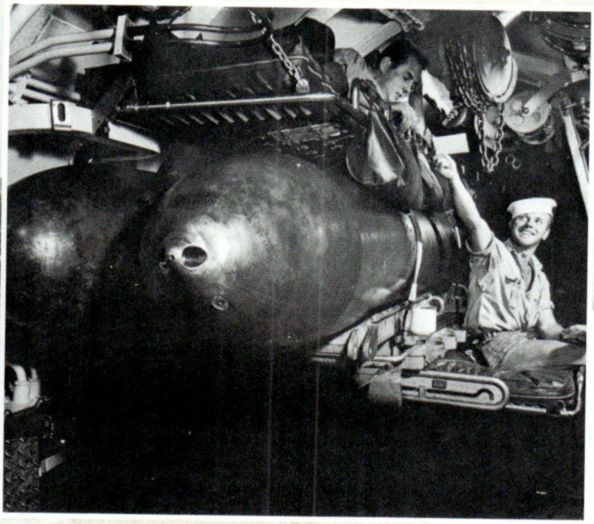

The submarines fired torpedoes to damage ships beneath the waterline. Conditions were so cramped that the crew slept among the torpedoes.

periscope: A tube fitted with mirrors that allows people in submarines to see the ocean surface.

The T-34 had relatively wide tracks. They helped it to cross soft ground and gave it greater freedom to maneuver.

T-34 Tank

The German army was shocked when it came across the T-34 in 1941 during the invasion of the Soviet Union. The Soviet tank had a high-velocity gun and an electrically operated turret. In addition, the turret armor was over 2 inches (52 mm) thick. Its tracks, the most **vulnerable** part of any tank, were easy to maintain. More that 40,000 T-34s were built. The T-34 remains the basic model for all subsequent battle tanks.

vulnerable: Open to attack or destruction.

A MATCH FOR THE PANZERS

The T-34's sloping armor made it difficult for German shells to score a direct hit. Meanwhile, its own 3-inch (76.2 mm) gun could destroy a German Panzer ("tank" in German) from outside the Panzer's range. The T-34 used fuel that was less flammable than that used by the U.S. Sherman tank, so it was less likely to catch fire if hit. Its wide tracks let it cross any kind of **terrain** without getting stuck in mud. The Germans were so impressed by the T-34 that they copied many of its features into the new tanks they began to produce in mid-1943 to take on the T-34.

GERMAN PANZERS

The German tactic of Blitzkrieg—"lightning war"—relied on Panzers. The first generation of Panzers broke through defenses and made rapid advances, backed up by aircraft, artillery, and infantry. Panzers stormed through Poland, France, Belgium, and the Netherlands. Before they met the T-34 in 1941, the German Panzers had been the supreme battlefield tanks of the war. After that, they had to be upgraded because they were outclassed.

A four-man crew poses with its T-34. The tank had a commander, a driver, a loader, and a gunner (in some models, the commander also had to fire the main gun).

terrain: The physical shape and characteristics of an area of ground.

Glossary

amphibious: Something that can operate on land or in the water.

armored fighting vehicle: A military vehicle protected by armor and equipped with weapons.

barrage: A large amount of shells or bombs delivered at the same time.

battleship: The most heavily armed type of warship.

bombardier: The member of a bomber crew whose job is to aim and drop the aircraft's bombs.

cockpit: The part of an airplane where the pilot and copilot sit.

conscripts: Untrained civilians who are forced to serve in the army.

firefight: A close-range gunfight in which both sides fire at the other.

ground crew: The mechanics who maintain an airplane and prepare it for flights.

howitzer: An artillery gun that fires shells in a high arc to pass over enemy defenses.

hydraulic: Powered by energy created by putting liquids under pressure.

magazine: A metal case loaded with a number of cartridges ready to be clipped into a machine gun.

merchant ship: An unarmed cargo vessel used for trade.

monoplane: An aircraft with one wing on either side.

occupied: Controlled by the enemy.

partisan: Someone who fights in a resistance group in occupied territory.

pressurized: Made safe and comfortable by pumping air in.

recoil: The force that pushes a gun backward when it fires.

reconnaissance: Gathering information by surveying enemy positions.

rocket: A missile that is powered by its own fuel and propulsion unit.

self-propelled: For guns, able to move on their own through the use of an engine and wheels or tracks.

strafe: To fire from the air at targets on the ground.

transport plane: An aircraft that is adapted to carry large amounts of cargo or soldiers.

Further Information

Allen, Sam. *U.S. Weapons of World War II*. Burgundy Cross, 2022.

Doeden, Matt. *Weapons of World War II*. Capstone, 2018.

Doyle, David. *The Complete Guide to German Armored Vehicles*. Skyhorse, 2019.

Eyewitness. *World War II.* Dorling Kindersley, 2021.

Halls, Kelly Milner. *World War II History for Kids (500 Facts).* Rockridge Press, 2021.

Jackson, Robert. *Warplanes of World War II*. Sterling Publishing, 2018.

Jordan, David and Andrew Wiest. *World War II Illustrated Atlas: Campaigns, Battles and Weapons*. Sterling Publishing, 2019.

McDonald, Clara. *Weapons of World War II*. North Star Editions, 2022.

Websites

https://www.militaryfactory.com/worldwar2/weapons.php
This site explores a big range of weapons from World War II.

https://www.archives.gov/research/alic/reference/military/ww2.html
The National Archives site contains information on a wide range of aviation weapons.

http://www.history-of-american-wars.com/world-war-2-weapons.html
This site includes a general overview, along with short entries on each weapon or weapons system.

https://www.thoughtco.com/world-war-ii-weapons-2361532
Browse a well-illustrated, comprehensive list of weapons used in the war.

Publisher's note to educators and parents: Our editors have carefully reviewed these websites to ensure that they are suitable for students. Many websites change frequently, however, and we cannot guarantee that a site's future contents will continue to meet our high standards of quality and educational value. Be advised that students should be closely supervised whenever they access the Internet.

Index